Easy Paper 

BOOK # 2

by Mary Currier

Home Ties
Specialties for the Homeschooling Family
3750 Middleburg, Rd, Union Bridge, MD 2179
410-775-2511   E-mail: hometies@juno.com

Christian Light Publications, Inc.
Harrisonburg, VA 22801

Christian Light Publications, Inc.,
Harrisonburg, Virginia 22801
© 1999 by Christian Light Publications, Inc.
All rights reserved. Published 1999
Printed in the United States of America

07 06 05 04 03 02 01 00 99   5 4 3 2 1

ISBN 0-87813-586-3

From the Publishers

We were gratified with the enthusiastic response of teachers and parents to *Easy Paper Crafts Book #1.* Now we are happy to present *Easy Paper Crafts Book #2,* with more inspirational projects for preschool through the early grades.

The 50 activities provide practice in coloring, cutting, folding, gluing, and displaying. Children learn to use their hands and follow directions as they make projects for personal satisfaction or gifts for others. Scriptural themes turn their minds toward God.

Common supplies and tools and easily followed instructions make it simple for Mom or teacher to have a craft time. Copying or gluing onto heavier paper will make sturdier projects.

We present these craft projects as **reproducible blackline masters,** permitting you to make multiple copies as needed for group use. This does not permit copying for sale or mass distribution, nor does this permission apply to other CLP publications unless specifically stated therein.

Christian Light Publications, Inc.
P.O. Box 1212
Harrisonburg, VA 22801-1212

Contents

Easy Models

Easy Games and Activities

Easy Decorative or Useful Items

Easy Mottoes, Plaques, and Posters

Easy Models

1. Basket of Apples

Materials needed:

— Two 8″ paper plates   — Glue
— Crayons   — Scissors

1. Cut out the inside of two plates as shown in example (1).
2. Place the plates together with the inside rims together.
3. Glue to hold.
4. Color to look like a basket.
5. Color and cut out the apple picture.
6. Set apple picture in the basket.
7. Use a black crayon and print "GOD SUPPLIES" on the handle.

(1)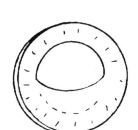

(2)

(3, 4)

2. Praying Boy

1. Color
2. Cut out.
3. Fold on dotted lines.
4. Set up.

3. Windsock — "God Made This Day"

1. Color.
2. Cut out on heavy lines.
3. Apply glue on tab.
4. Roll to form a tube shape and fasten.
5. Tie a 12-inch length of string in holes to hang.

God
Made This Day

Apply glue here.

4. Fall Leaf Mobile

1. Color leaves using fall colors.
2. Color acorns brown.
3. Apply glue to tab of mobile.
4. Fasten to form a tube shape.
5. Tie leaves at various lengths as shown.

*Variation:
   Spread an even layer of glue over leaves.
   Then sprinkle ground cinnamon over glue.
   Shake off excess.

In everything
give thanks.

Tab

5. Dove of Peace

God gives real peace.

1. Cut out the square below.
2. Fold diagonally to center.
3. Fold as shown.
4. Attach string at proper location to balance horizontally and hang as a mobile.

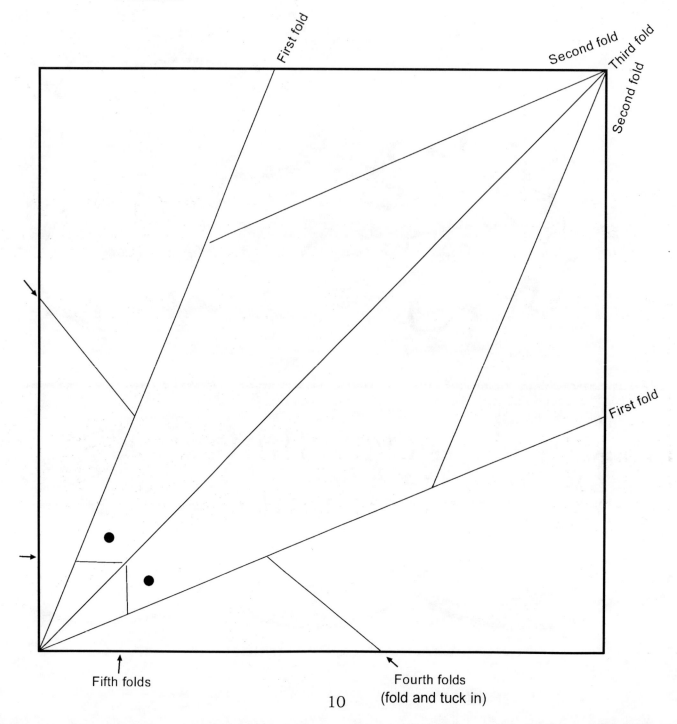

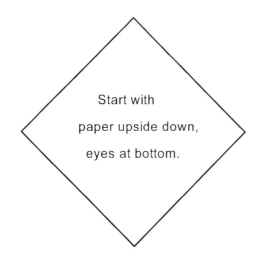

Start with
paper upside down,
eyes at bottom.

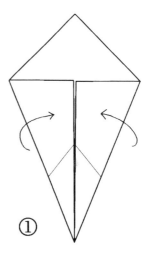

①

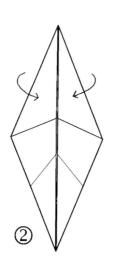

②

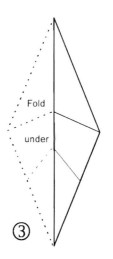

Fold

under

③

④

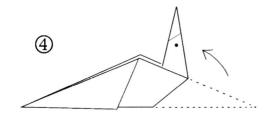

⑤

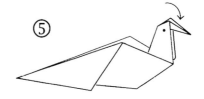

6. Black-Capped Chickadee

1. Glue patterns onto cardboard.
2. Cut out.
3. Fold on dotted lines.
4. Insert wings into slot in bird's body.
5. Punch holes where shown.
6. Tie a 10-inch length of thread or string in holes to hang up.

God takes
care of us.

7. Stuffed Fish

1. Color fish pieces.
2. Cut out.
3. Apply glue to all the outer edges on the inside except the tail. Glue an 8-inch piece of string in the fish's mouth.
4. Stuff with crumpled facial tissue up to the tail. Then glue the tail together.

Jesus said: "Follow me, and I will make you fishers of men."

Matthew 4:19

8. Pumpkin

1. Color pumpkin orange, stem brown, and leaf green.
2. Cut out on heavy, outside lines.
3. Fold on dotted lines.
4. Form the pumpkin by bringing the points together and gluing in place.
5. Apply glue on tab of stem and stick on top of the pumpkin.

GREAT IS
THE LORD

Great
is the
Lord

stem

TAB

pumpkin

17

9. Elephant

1. Color project.
2. Cut out on outside lines.
3. Fold on dotted lines.
4. Glue together as shown.
5. Stand up.

God will
give you
strength

19

10. Timely Advice for Boys

1. Color the project pieces on this page and the next a pale yellow (or use a copy machine and make copies using yellow or light gold paper).
2. Cut out on outer lines and inside rings where indicated.
3. Fold on dotted lines.
4. Slip the clock pieces inside the folding clock. Staple or glue together in the ring area only.
5. Make a chain from the strips on the following page and fasten to pocket watch.

CUT OUT

CUT OUT

CUT OUT

CUT OUT

Only one life
T'will soon be past,
Only what's done
For Christ will last.

"Watch and Pray,"
Matthew 26:41

- The Lord watches over you.
- Take time to read the Bible.
- Lost time is never found again.—(Ben Franklin)
- Do not waste your time.

Timely Advice
Watch how you act!

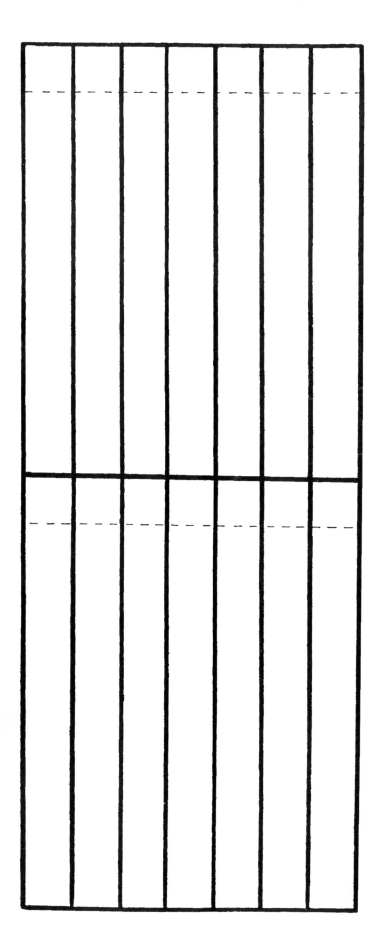

CUT OUT

- Watch what you say.
- Use your time wisely.
- It is time to seek the Lord.
- Watch for Christ's return.
- Time is running out. Don't waste it.

CUT OUT

The clock of
Life is wound but once,
And no man has the power
To tell just when the
hands will stop
At late or early hour.
Now is the only time you own,
Live, love, toil with a will.
Place no faith in
tomorrow, for the
clock may then
be still.

11. Blessing Bees

1. Color project pieces.
2. Cut out.
3. Fold bee's wings.
4. Glue strips hanging down from flower as shown.
5. Glue bees on flower and strips.

24

12. Watch

1. Color the "watch."
2. Cut out on heavy lines.
3. Cut two slits on the buckle where shown.
4. Slip on the child's wrist.
5. Tighten to fit by putting bottom side of band into slits.
6. Glue to hold if desired.

Watch
how
you
spend
your
time!

13. Useful Donkey

1. Color project pieces.
2. Cut out on heavy lines.
3. Fasten together with brass fasteners.

Donkeys were used in Bible times as surefooted animals for carrying things.

Be a helper in the ways you can.

Be a helper
in the ways
you can.

14. Indoor Boomerang

1. Cut out.
2. Glue to lightweight cardboard. Cut out again.
3. Bend tips slightly.
4. Throw and watch it come back to you.

YOUR ACTIONS WILL

TREAT OTHERS THE WAY YOU WANT TO BE TREATED.

COME BACK TO YOU.

15. Kitten

Kittens and cats are usually known for being clean and gentle.

To make:
1. Color the kitten's nose, tongue, and ribbon.
2. Cut out on the outside lines.
3. Glue fluffed-up cotton balls over the kitten's body, tail, and legs. Let dry.
4. Apply glue to tab and roll kitten in a cone shape and fasten.
5. If desired, glue more fluffed-out cotton on the other side of the tail.

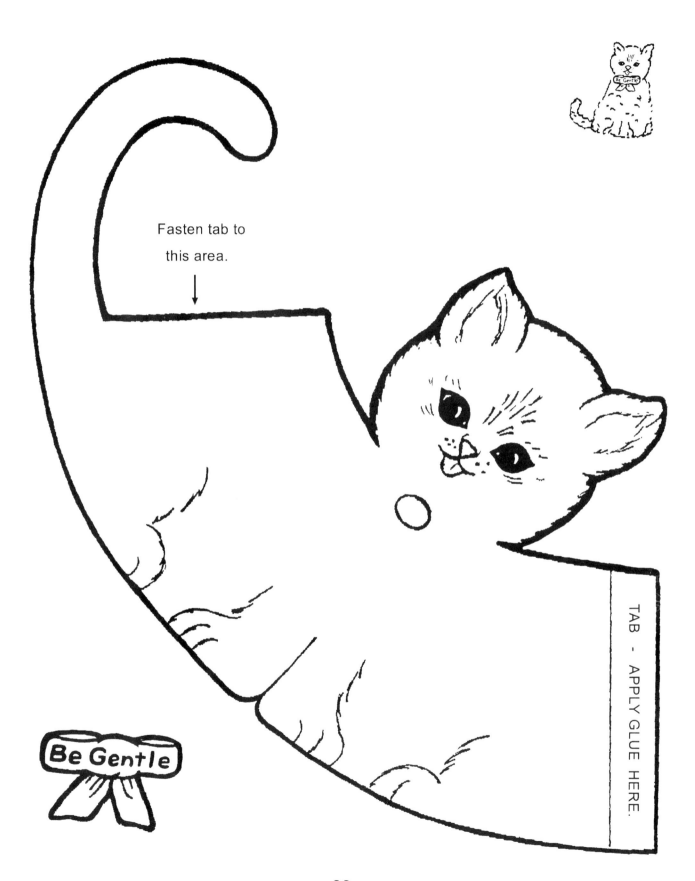

Fasten tab to this area.

Be Gentle

TAB - APPLY GLUE HERE.

Easy Games
and Activities

16. "God Is Now Here" Word Lesson

To make:
1. Cut out word strips on the next page.
2. Glue together on tab.
3. Fold a pleat in sign, bringing mark after the s forward to the mark after o, and hiding the letters n o.
4. Use in the following story:

Story:

Hannah's schoolteacher did not believe in God. He would mock and make fun of the Bible. He wanted to put doubt in the minds of those in the classroom. On the wall he put up a sign that said, "GOD IS WHERE?" (show word strip to show this.) He wanted to question anyone who did believe in God.

Hannah raised her hand. When the teacher called on her, she quietly told him that God was everywhere.

The next day he put up another sign that said "GOD IS NOWHERE" (show word strip with pleat opened and question mark folded to back). He was upset that anyone would question what he said and wanted to teach the children that there was no God. Angrily he hit his desk with his fist.

"How could anyone believe in a God no one can see?" he demanded. In rage he took his pencil to point to the sign he had put up. Accidently, his pencil ripped the sign. (At this point tear the sign between the letters W and H.) Unknown to him the sign now had a new meaning. It now read "GOD IS NOW HERE." In his anger, the teacher had made the sign answer his question about where God was.

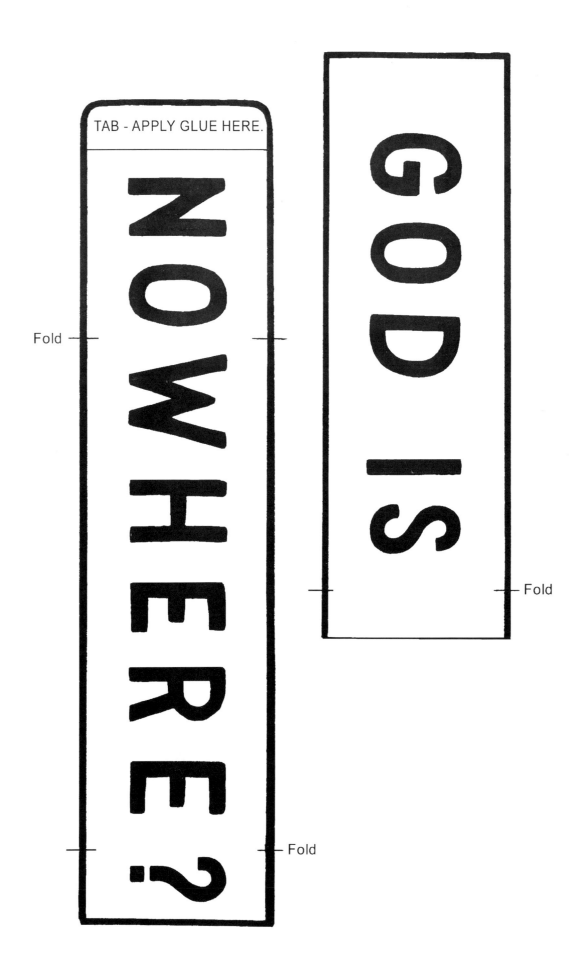

TAB - APPLY GLUE HERE.

Fold

Fold

Fold

NOWHERE?

GOD IS

37

17. "God Made Everything" Puzzle

1. Color picture.
2. Cut out pieces. Have fun trying to put the pieces back together.

*If desired, glue on lightweight cardboard and cut out again.

18. Kinds of Books

Most books today are made of sheets of paper which are stapled or bound together at one side, making a front and a back cover. Many years ago there were other ways books were made.

Clay tablets were used in Bible times. These dried tablets are preserved even now.

Scrolls were used for thousands of years. Silk, skins of animals, and plant strips were also used.

Wooden tablets were used by the Chinese. These were long, thin strips that were printed with clay seals.

The folded book, as the one you are making, was used in China in the 800-900's and is still used in some lands today.

To make:
1. Cut out the project.
2. Read the story and draw your own pictures to fit the story.
3. Fold on the dotted lines to form a fold-out booklet.

The wise and foolish builders

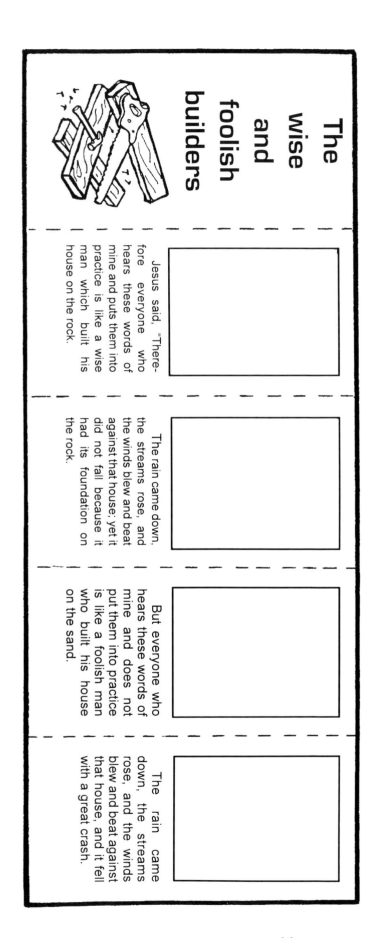

Jesus said, "Therefore everyone who hears these words of mine and puts them into practice is like a wise man which built his house on the rock.

The rain came down, the streams rose, and the winds blew and beat against that house; yet it did not fall because it had its foundation on the rock.

But everyone who hears these words of mine and does not put them into practice is like a foolish man who built his house on the sand.

The rain came down, the streams rose, and the winds blew and beat against that house, and it fell with a great crash.

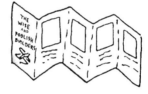

19. Owl Bible Memory Activity

1. Color owl and cut out. Fold on dotted lines and glue as shown.
2. Cut out Bible memory cards and look up those references in your Bible. Print the verses on the back side of each card.
3. Place cards in the owl's box and memorize the verses.

*If desired, make more cards with Bible verses to memorize.

Matthew 24:42	Proverbs 15:3	Psalm 19:14
	Psalm 119:1	Proverbs 8:17
Matthew 5:40	Psalm 51:17	Psalm 9:17
Isaiah 55:6	Genesis 17:1	Genesis 28:5

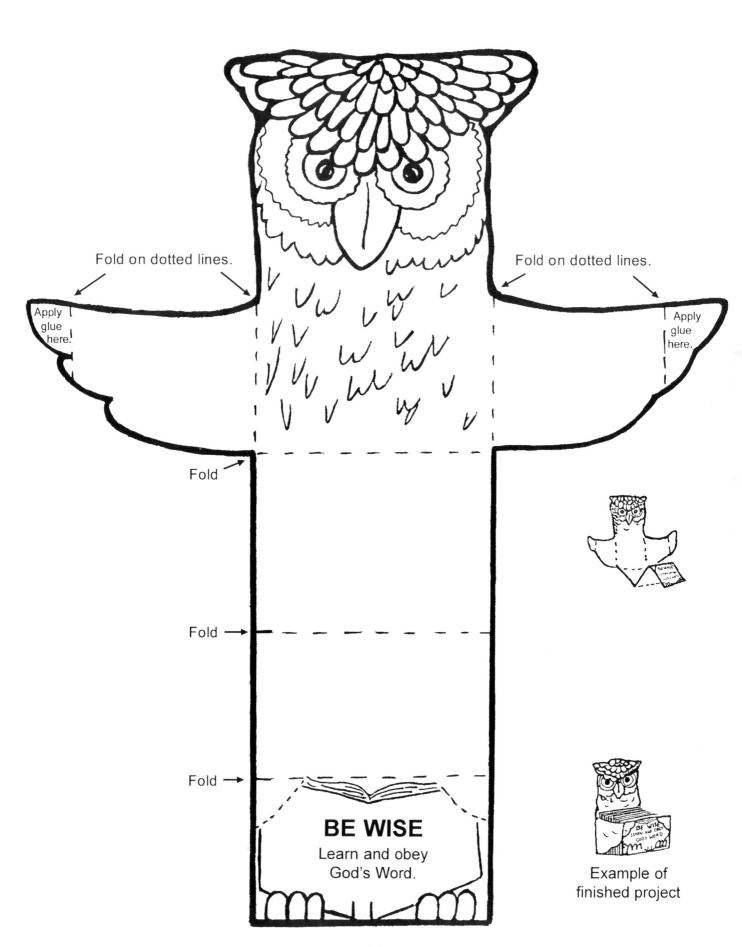

Fold on dotted lines.

Apply glue here.

Fold on dotted lines.

Apply glue here.

Fold

Fold

Fold

BE WISE

Learn and obey God's Word.

Example of finished project

20. Obey the Shepherd Game

1. Color the game on this page and the next.
2. Cut out sheep markers and fold on dotted lines.
3. Cut out game board and glue together where indicated.
4. Find a friend or two to help you play the game.

To play:
— Each player uses one sheep marker.
— Choose one player to go first.
— Flip a coin — head move 2 spaces and tails move 1 space. Then follow any additional rules on some spaces.
— The player that reaches the sheepfold first wins the game.

START

Caught in a thorn bush. Go back 1 space.

Came when the shepherd called. Go ahead 3 spaces.

Stayed close to the shepherd. Take another turn.

Took a long time getting a drink. Lose a turn.

Thought you heard it thunder. Go back to start.

Fell in the pond. Go back 3 spaces.

sheep markers

Wooly

Snowball

Frisky

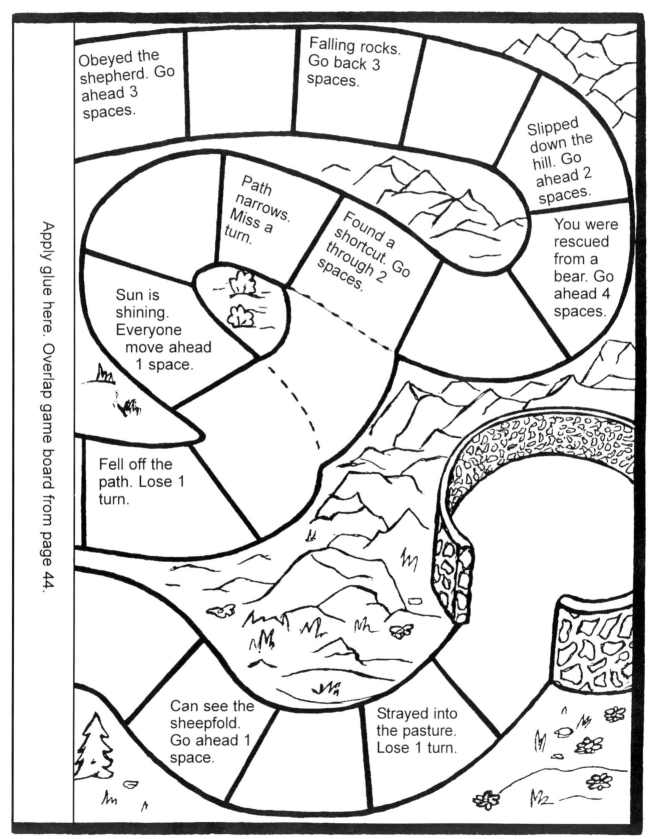

21. "Be Thankful" Game

1. Cut out game.
2. Fold on dotted lines in order shown.
3. Give the game to a friend to play.

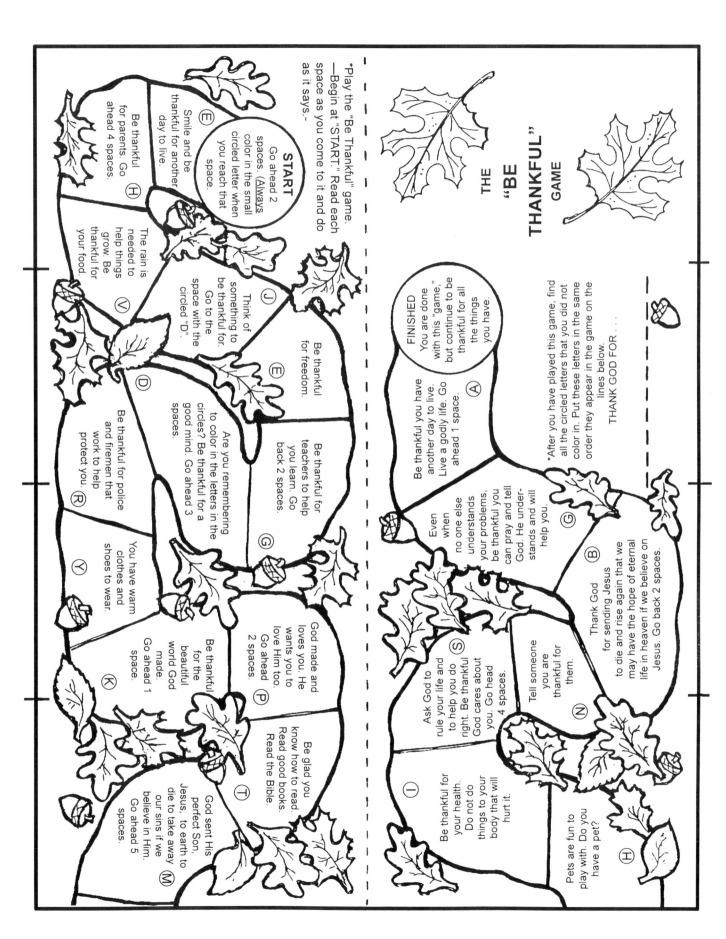

THE "BE THANKFUL" GAME

*Play the "Be Thankful" game.
—Begin at "START." Read each space as you come to it and do as it says.-

START
Go ahead 2 spaces. (Always color in the small circled letter when you reach that space.

(H) Smile and be thankful for another day to live.

(E) Be thankful for parents. Go ahead 4 spaces.

(V) The rain is needed to help things grow. Be thankful for your food.

(J) Think of something to be thankful for. Go to the space with the circled "D."

(E) Be thankful for freedom.

(E) Be thankful for teachers to help you learn. Go back 2 spaces.

(D) Are you remembering to color in the letters in the circles? Be thankful for a good mind. Go ahead 3 spaces.

(R) Be thankful for police and firemen that work to help protect you.

(G) God made and loves you. He wants you to love Him too. Go ahead 2 spaces.

(Y) You have warm clothes and shoes to wear.

(P) Be thankful for the beautiful world God made. Go ahead 1 space.

(T) Be glad you know how to read. Read good books. Read the Bible.

(K) God sent His perfect Son, Jesus, to earth to die to take away our sins if we believe in Him. Go ahead 5 spaces.

(M)

FINISHED
You are done with this "game," but continue to be thankful for all the things you have.

(A) Be thankful you have another day to live. Live a godly life. Go ahead 1 space.

*After you have played this game, find all the circled letters that you did not color in. Put these letters in the same order they appear in the game on the lines below.
THANK GOD FOR . . . .

Even when no one else understands your problems, be thankful you can pray and tell God. He understands and will help you.

(G)

(B) Thank God for sending Jesus to die and rise again that we may have the hope of eternal life in heaven if we believe on Jesus. Go back 2 spaces.

(S) Ask God to rule your life and to help you do right. Be thankful God cares about you. Go head 4 spaces.

(N) Tell someone you are thankful for them.

(I) Be thankful for your health. Do not do things to your body that will hurt it.

(H) Pets are fun to play with. Do you have a pet?

47

22. "Defeat the Devil" Word Lesson

Everyone is tempted to do wrong. Temptation is not sin, but giving in to it is. With God's help we can overcome sin. Use this object lesson as a reminder of how to defeat the devil.

Cut out the word cards. Fold on the dotted lines to get ready for the lesson.

Lesson:
— Read 1 Corinthians 10:13.
— (Show the word DEVIL). The devil, also called Satan, tempts everyone. He is the author of all evil and a powerful enemy. His business is to DO EVIL (stretch out the word DEVIL to the DO EVIL position). He wants you to DO EVIL too.
— There is only one way to defeat the devil. It is by using GOD'S WORD (show card). This weapon is also called a SWORD (fold back card to show word). (Read Ephesians 6:17). The Word of God is powerful and the only weapon to defeat the devil (Hebrews 4:12).

GOD'S

WORD

DO

EVIL

49

Becoming a Missionary

When someone decides to be a missionary, time is spent preparing. The language, customs, and people are studied. A missionary needs to know the climate, foods, and dress.

Let's learn some things about Ireland as if you were going to be a missionary there.

Ireland is a small island country in the continent of Europe. It has rolling, green farmlands and mild, wet weather. They grow potatoes, grains, and animals. The people of Ireland are friendly and have close families. They eat simple foods. Most of them go to the Roman Catholic church.

23. Irish Soda Bread

Potatoes, mutton (sheep meat) and apples are common foods in Ireland. Traditional meals include potato soup, lamb and potato stew, spiced apple tarts, and soda bread.

Irish Soda Bread

4 cups whole wheat flour
2 cups white flour
1¼ cups sour milk
1 teaspoon soda
1 teaspoon salt

Mix the flour, soda, and salt together. Make a hole in the ingredients and add the milk. Mix lightly and quickly. If dough is too stiff, add more milk but not to make a wet dough.

Put a small amount of flour on the counter. Put the dough on the flour and pat dough to make a flattened circle about 1½ inches thick. Place on a baking sheet and make a large cross with a floured knife. Bake at 375 degrees for 40 minutes. (Test if it is done by putting a knife gently in the center of the bread. If the knife comes out clean, it is done.) To keep the bread soft, wrap in a clean towel.

24. Flag Pencil Topper

1. Color the flag of Ireland as indicated.
2. Cut out on solid heavy lines.
3. Apply glue behind area indicated and fasten together.
4. Slip on end of pencil.

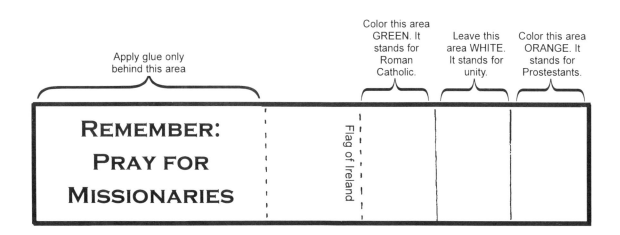

Apply glue only
behind this area

Color this area
GREEN. It
stands for
Roman
Catholic.

Leave this
area WHITE.
It stands for
unity.

Color this area
ORANGE. It
stands for
Prostestants.

REMEMBER:

PRAY FOR

MISSIONARIES

Flag of Ireland

IRELAND

DUBLIN

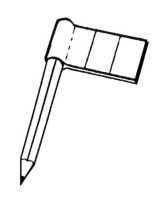

25. Gaelic Word Tickets

Missionaries often need to learn another language to teach in other countries. Some languages are very hard to learn.

Gaelic is considered difficult to learn. It was spoken in Ireland long ago. Most people in Ireland speak English today but some still speak the Gaelic language.

The following are some Gaelic words and their meanings. Use them as a code to figure out the meaning of the tickets. Then cut out the tickets and do what they say.

Luan — Monday
Mairt — Tuesday
Céadaoin — Wednesday
Déar daoin — Thursday
Aoine — Friday
Sathairn — Saturday
Domhrach — Sunday
Teach — house
Máthar — mother
Athar — father
Cistin — kitchen
Bainne — milk
Úl — apple
Sea — yes
Deas — right
Scoil — school
Codladh sámh — goodnight
Eaglais — church
Múinteoir — teacher

Eitleán — airplane
Leaoa — bed
Fear — man
Deirfiúr — sister
Dearthár — brother
Aon (oon) — one
Dha (yah) — two
Tri (try) — three
Ceithir (kay hyur) — four
Coig (coh egg) — five
Se (shee) — six
Seachd (siry ahch) — seven
Ochd (ahch) — eight
Naoid (noo eh ee) — nine
Deich (deeyah esh) — ten

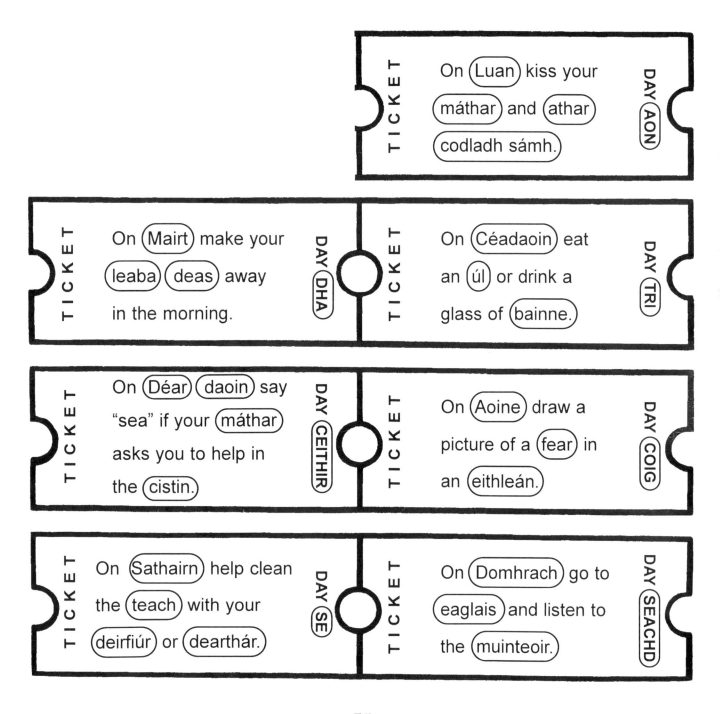

TICKET — On (Luan) kiss your (máthar) and (athar) codladh sámh. — **DAY (AON)**

TICKET — On (Mairt) make your (leaba) (deas) away in the morning. — **DAY (DHA)**

TICKET — On (Céadaoin) eat an (úl) or drink a glass of (bainne.) — **DAY (TRI)**

TICKET — On (Déar) (daoin) say "sea" if your (máthar) asks you to help in the (cistin.) — **DAY (CEITHIR)**

TICKET — On (Aoine) draw a picture of a (fear) in an (eithleán.) — **DAY (COIG)**

TICKET — On (Sathairn) help clean the (teach) with your (deirfiúr) or (dearthár.) — **DAY (SE)**

TICKET — On (Domhrach) go to (eaglais) and listen to the (muinteoir.) — **DAY (SEACHD)**

Irish enjoy riddles, jokes, and sayings. Some of them are common to us. For example, sayings like "March comes in like a lion and goes out like a lamb," and "You cannot find a thing except in the place it is" are Irish sayings. Some of the sayings have about the same meanings as Bible verses. Examples are: "Don't count your chicks before they are hatched" (Proverbs 27:1); "Never put off until tomorrow what you can do today" (Proverbs 10:5); "If you are kind to your parents, you will have a long life" (Exodus 20:12); "Be as busy as a bee" (Proverbs 6:6); and "A full cabin is better than an empty castle" (Proverbs 14:4).

26. Irish Wall Plaque

1. Color project.
2. Cut out on outside lines.
3. Fold on dotted lines.
4. Apply glue to tabs and fasten to make a 3-D frame.
5. Make a hanger by taping a short length of string in a loop behind the picture.

*To make a more sturdy picture, glue lightweight cardboard behind picture and then cut out again.

Never put off until tomorrow what you can do today.

—OLD IRISH SAYING

TAB

TAB

TAB

TAB

27. Shamrock Sewing Card

The shamrock is Ireland's national flower. It is a three-leaf clover and was used by St. Patrick to help explain the Trinity to the Irish people.

To Make: Shamrock Sewing Card
1. Color project.
2. Cut out.
3. Glue to lightweight cardboard and cut out again. Use a paper punch to make holes in the dots of the shamrock.
4. Use green yarn through holes to lace up card.

FATHER

GOD

SON

SPIRIT

THE TRINITY

60

Who Is the Real "St. Patrick"?

The month of March reminds one of "St. Patrick's Day." Many stories have been told about him. Some stories are true but many are not. The best place to find out what he was like is to read what he wrote himself.

He would be surprised to know that he is called "St. Patrick." He was a humble man trying to obey God's calling by telling the Irish people about the true God. He never mentioned being part of the Roman Catholic church or being blessed by the pope. He gives God the glory as he writes, "I am greatly a debtor to God, who has bestowed His grace so largely upon me, that multitudes were born again to God through me. The Irish, who had never had the knowledge of God and worshiped only idols and unclean things, have lately become the people of the Lord, and are called sons of God."[1]

Patrick was born around 389 A.D. in Roman Britain. At the age of 41 or 42 he went to Ireland to evangelize the country. He was a hardworking missionary who saw thousands converted.

On March 17, somewhere between 461 and 493, he died.

1. "Patrick of Ireland" by Christa G. Habegger, March 1981, Faith for the Family, Bob Jones Press, Greenville, South Carolina.

28. Bible Objects Card Game

1. Color the pictures on this page and the next.
2. Glue to lightweight cardboard.
3. Cut out on all lines.
4. Play the game with a friend (or friends).

How to play:
1. Mix the cards, upside down.
2. Each player draws an equal number of cards.
3. Lay one card, face up, on the center of the table.
4. Players take turns drawing a card from the other players. If a player picks a card that matches the card on the table, he keeps the set. Then he draws another card from the next player and lays it face up on the table. He draws again from the next player to see whether he can form a set. His turn continues as long as he is forming sets.
5. The winner is the player with the most completed sets.

Easy Decorative or Useful Items

29. Wall Pocket

1. Color project.
2. Cut out.
3. Fold on dotted lines.
4. Apply glue to tabs and fasten to form a pocket.
5. Cut out the hole and tie a ribbon bow to hang up.
6. Fill with silk or dried flowers. Hang up.

30. Thanksgiving Napkin Rings

1. Color the project pieces on next page.
2. Cut out on heavy lines.
3. Cut tubes from paper towels or toilet paper into 1-inch lengths.
4. Glue paper project pieces around tube lengths.
5. Fold table napkins and insert in ring.
6. Place at table settings.

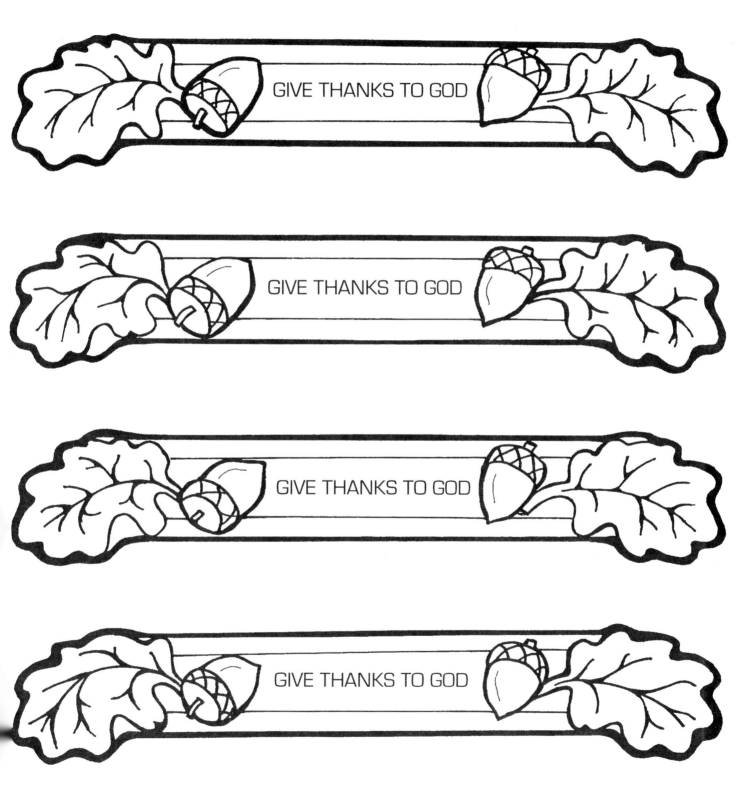

GIVE THANKS TO GOD

GIVE THANKS TO GOD

GIVE THANKS TO GOD

GIVE THANKS TO GOD

31. Nut Cup Basket

1. Color project.
2. Cut out on outside lines.
3. Fold on dotted lines.
4. Apply glue to tabs and press together to fasten.
5. Glue handle in place.
6. Fill with candy and nuts.

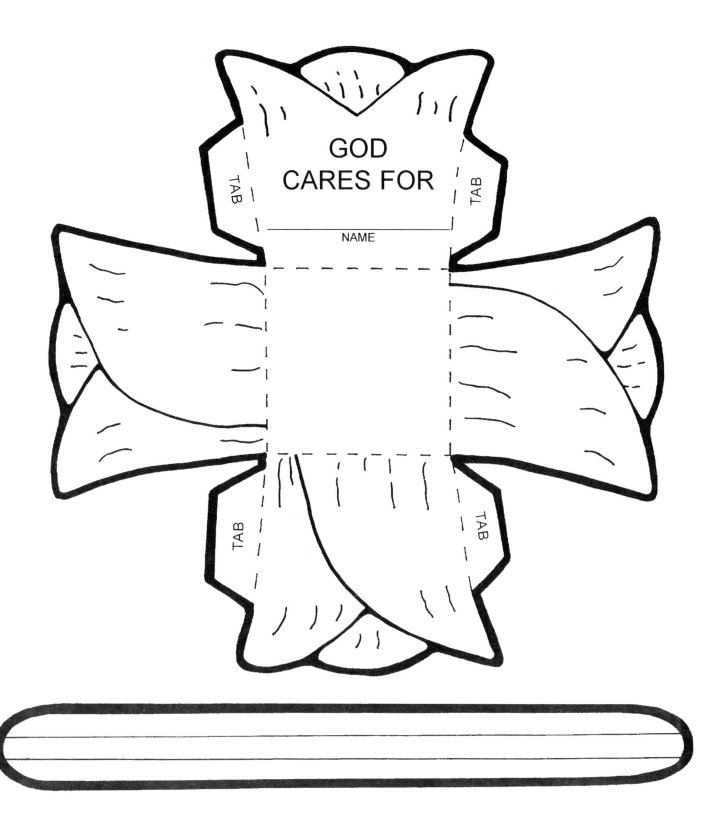

GOD
CARES FOR

TAB

TAB

NAME

TAB

TAB

32. Pencil Holder

1. Color project.
2. Cut out.
3. Apply glue behind project and wrap around an empty, 12 oz. frozen juice can.
4. Set up and use for a pencil holder.

HAPPINESS STARTS WITH A CONTENTED HEART.

"But godliness with contentment is great gain."
1 Timothy 6:6

33. Tract Holder

1. Glue on cardboard.
2. Cut out.
3. Fold on dotted lines.
4. Apply glue on tabs and fasten to form a pocket.
5. Punch holes and hang up with string.

JESUS IS THE ONLY WAY TO HEAVEN

- Repent and turn from all your sins.
- Believe that Jesus died on the cross as your only Saviour.
- Live a godly life.
- Trust God and obey His Word.

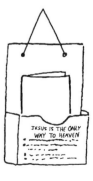

34. Wallet

1. Color.
2. Cut out on heavy lines and slit.
3. Fold on dotted lines.
4. Close by pushing tab into slit.

First fold

Second fold

IN GOD
WE
TRUST

Your name

Address

Phone number

Learn to be
saving. "A penny
saved is a
penny earned."

Lay up for yourselves
treasures in heaven.

IN GOD
WE
TRUST

35. Nut Basket

1. Color projects. Print names where shown.*
2. Cut out.
3. Fold on dotted lines.
4. Glue in place.
5. Fill with candy and nuts (you may want to put a small cupcake liner in the basket first to prevent oil getting on basket).
6. Put on Thanksgiving table as nameplates.

*You may want to copy more baskets if you have many guests.

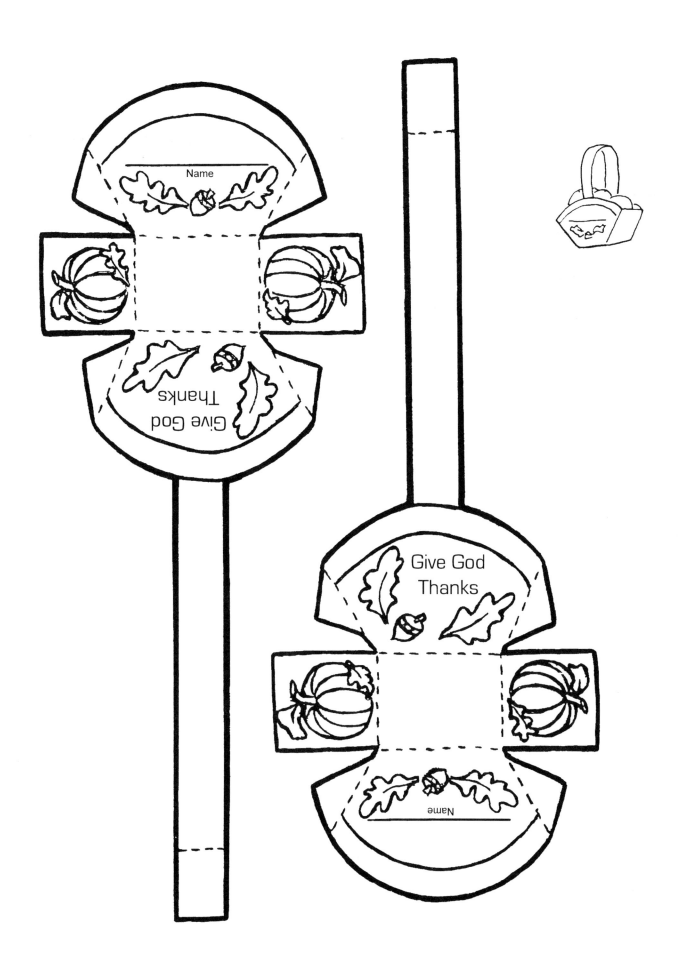

36. Napkin Ring

1. Color project pieces.
2. Cut out on outside lines.
3. Fold on dotted lines.
4. Cut a 2-inch length of tube (such as a bathroom tissue roll). Glue parts of turkey to tube as shown.

In the turkey feathers: IN EVERYTHING GIVE THANKS UNTO THE LORD OUR GOD.

37. Cupcake Decorations

1. Color.
2. Cut out.
3. Tape or glue a toothpick behind hearts.
4. Insert in tops of cupcakes.

GOD IS LOVE

A FRIEND IS A GIFT FROM GOD

LOVE THE LORD

LOVE OTHERS

JESUS LOVES YOU

LOVE IS FROM GOD

38. Sundial

1. Color.
2. Cut out.
3. Fold on dotted lines.
4. Apply glue behind tab.
5. Glue marker to sundial.
6. Glue project to bottom of paper plate.

*TO USE:
   Place the number XII (12) toward the north.

Example

Apply glue here.

Use your time wisely.

Lost time is never found.

Only what you do for God will last.

Easy Mottoes, Plaques, and Posters

39. Give Thanks

1. Color project.
2. Cut out.
3. Glue on thick cardboard. Cut out again.
4. Punch hole.
5. Cover project with a thin layer of glue. Immediately sprinkle white granulated sugar or clear glitter over picture. Shake off excess.
6. Hang up.

40. "My God Shall Supply Your Need" Plaque

Materials needed:
　　Cardboard from an old cereal box (or cardboard of like thickness)
　　Pretty cotton fabric, 10½" x 4½"
　　Scissors
　　Glue

Trace the pattern on the next page onto the cardboard and cut out.

Lay the fabric on a table with the back side up. Then place the cardboard in the center. Apply glue near the edge of the cardboard. Fold fabric around cardboard and press on the glued area. Hold until dry.

When dry, fold in the places as shown on the pattern. Apply glue on the tab area and fasten as shown.

When dry, cut out the verse on next page and glue on one side of the plaque. (If desired, glue small decorations around the Bible verse.)

For a variation, print your own favorite Bible verse on a piece of paper about the size in this project and glue that on the plaque.

"My God
shall
supply
all
your
need."

41. Desktop Nameplate

Life is short. No one knows what tomorrow will bring. Seek God early in life. Live a godly life that is pure and separated from wickedness. Ask God for wisdom to know right from wrong. Use every minute wisely. Do not waste your time doing nothing or seeking empty pleasure. Someday you will give account to God for how you lived here on earth. Don't be a fool!

Make a Desktop Nameplate
1. Print your name in the box.
2. Color the rest of the project.
3. Cut out.
4. Fold on lines marked with arrows.
5. Apply glue to tab.
6. Form in triangle shape. Set on desk.

JOHN JONES

EVERY DAY IS A GIFT FROM GOD.

"Teach us to number our days."

Psalm 90:12

APPLY GLUE HERE.

93

42. Prayer Plaque

Even a child can learn to pray. Remember, you are talking to God who made and controls everything. Thank Him for all the good things He gave you. Ask God for help in obeying the Bible and living a godly life. Pray wisely. Think of other people's needs, and what you could do for them that would please God.

To make:
1. Color the project.
2. Cut out.
3. Fold on dotted line.
4. Set up.

Example of
finished project.

Now I lay me down to sleep,
I pray Thee, Lord, my soul to keep.
If I die before I wake,
I pray Thee, Lord, my soul to take.

43. Schooltime Banner

1. Color project pieces.
2. Cut out on outside lines.
3. Fold on dotted lines.
4. Apply glue on back side of banner pieces at the tips.
5. Insert a long string or yarn through all flags in order to spell
   S-C-H-O-O-L-T-I-M-E.
6. Hang up.

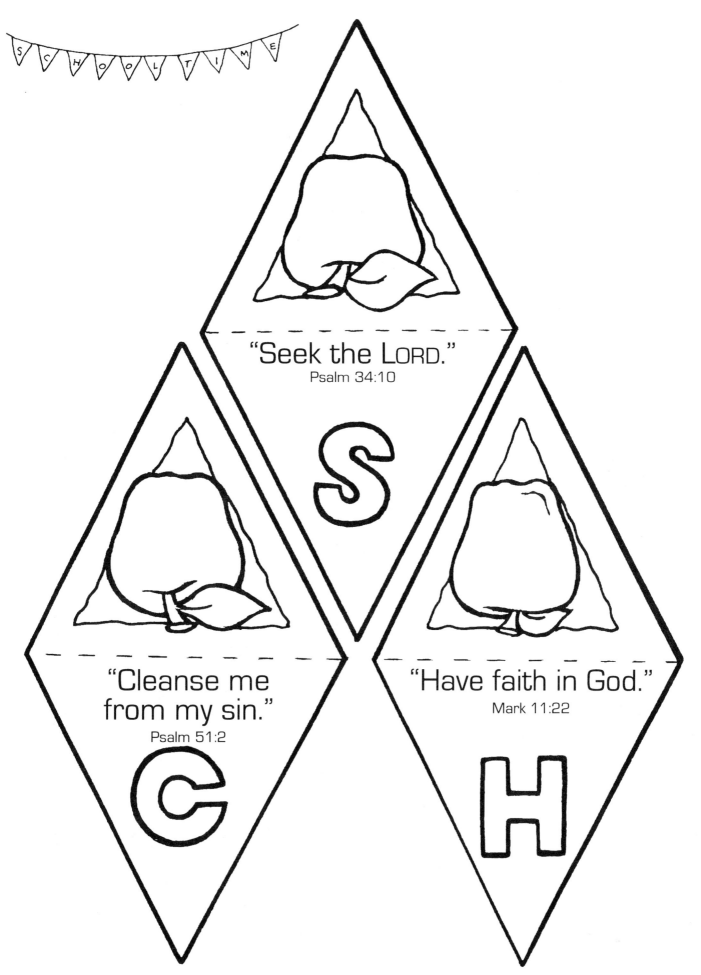

"Seek the LORD."
Psalm 34:10

S

"Cleanse me
from my sin."
Psalm 51:2

C

"Have faith in God."
Mark 11:22

H

97

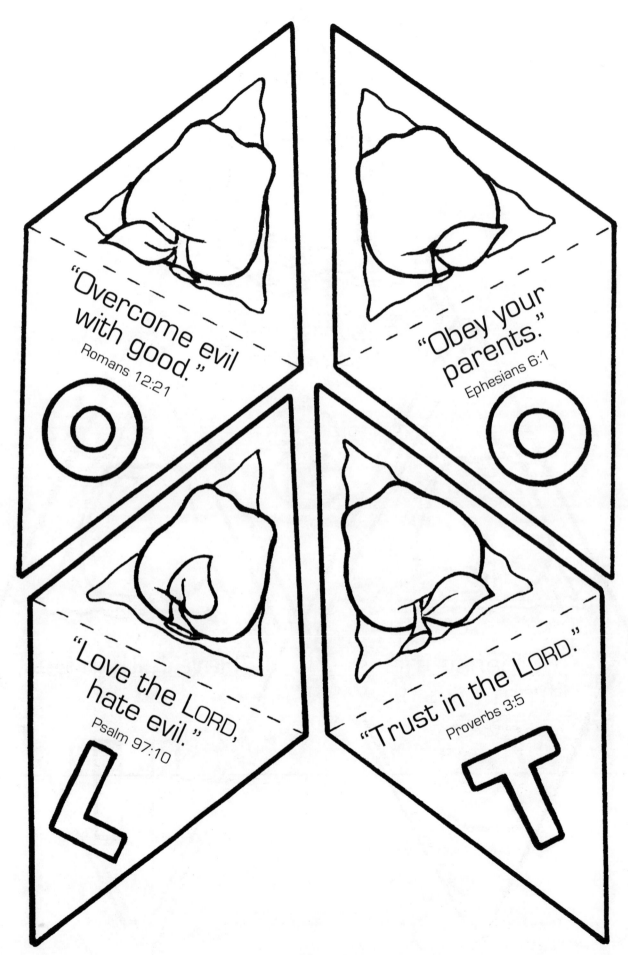

"Overcome evil with good."
Romans 12:21

"Obey your parents."
Ephesians 6:1

"Love the LORD, hate evil."
Psalm 97:10

"Trust in the LORD."
Proverbs 3:5

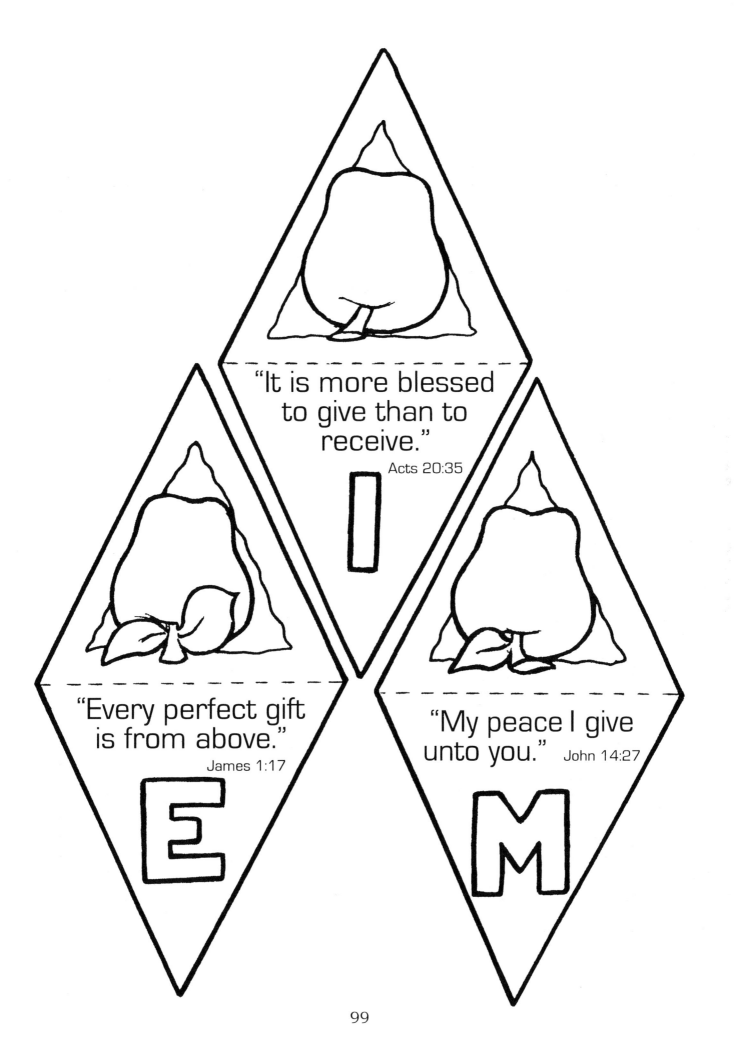

"It is more blessed
to give than to
receive."

Acts 20:35

I

"Every perfect gift
is from above."

James 1:17

E

"My peace I give
unto you." John 14:27

M

99

44. Swan Plaque

1. Cut out project on heavy, black lines.
2. Color the inside of a paper plate light blue.
3. Glue the project to the back of another paper plate. Then cut out again.
4. Glue the paper plate with the swan to the plate colored blue, with the rims together.
5. Add a string to hang.

The peace of God... passes all understanding.

45. Apple Wall Decoration

1. Color project pieces.
2. Cut out on outside, heavy lines.
3. Lay the two strips vertically on a flat surface.
4. Glue parts of the apple onto the strips as shown.

46. Mini-Plaque or Magnet

1. Color leaves and flower.
2. Cut out project pieces.
3. Lay a piece of corrugated cardboard (a 2½ in. by 2½ in. square) on the center of a piece of fabric (4½ in. by 5 in. square of small-printed cotton cloth). Make sure the back side of the fabric is facing up.
4. Glue the cardboard onto the cloth; fold sides of cloth up as if you were wrapping a gift; glue. When dry, turn over and glue the folded side down onto the lace pattern.
5. Glue the verse onto the center of the cloth-covered cardboard. Glue the flower and leaves on one corner around the verse.
6. Apply a 2-inch strip of self-adhesive magnetic tape behind the plaque to use as a magnet.

*Variations:
1. Color paper lace if desired.
2. Use small-print wallpaper scraps instead of fabric; use gift wrap or self-sticking plastic.
3. Instead of magnetic tape, use a short length of string or yarn and glue to the back as a hanger.
4. Use about one foot of real lace instead of paper lace. (Use 100% cotton lace if possible). Then glue a 2½ in. by 2½ in. lightweight cardboard piece behind lace.
5. Use silk or dried flowers instead of paper.
6. Use store-bought doily instead of the paper lace.

 Lay cardboard on <u>back</u> side of cloth.

 Fold and glue firmly.

 Turn over and glue on verse.

 Add flower and leaves in corner.

 Glue firmly onto lace.

Jesus never fails!

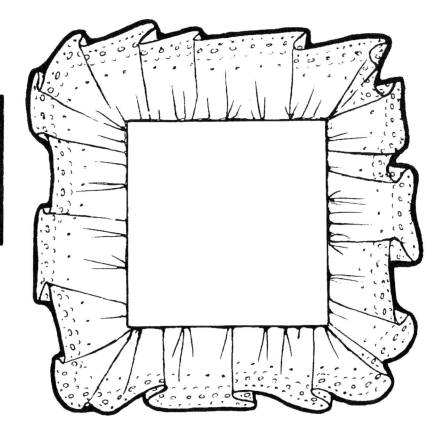

47. Fall Wreath

1. Color project pieces using the code.
2. Cut out pieces on heavy lines.
3. Apply glue in area marked with a *.
4. Place stem end of leaves in glue.
5. Place nuts on top.

CODE:

1 = green

2 = tan

3 = dark brown

4 = yellow

Praise the
Lord for His
goodness.

48. Open Bible Plaque

1. Color pictures on the Project Piece A.
2. Cut out A and fold on dotted line.
3. Color Project Piece B brown. Glue it onto cardboard or copy it onto stiff paper.
4. Cut out B and fold on dotted line to form a plaque stand.
5. Cut out Project Piece C.
6. Fold C on dotted lines. Glue back sides together. (Holy Bible will be visible on one side and the 3 glue strips on the otehr.)
7. Apply glue on strips indicated on C.
8. Glue the back of A to C as follows:
   a. Center of A to center strip of C.
   b. Outside edges of A to outside strips of C.
      (Each side of A will have a slight bow.)
9. Color D (suggested color: gold, yellow, or purple). Cut out.
10. Glue D onto Bible as shown.
11. Set Bible on plaque stand.

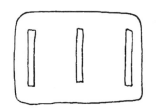

A →

"Believe that Jesus died and rose again."

I Thessalonians 4:14

B →

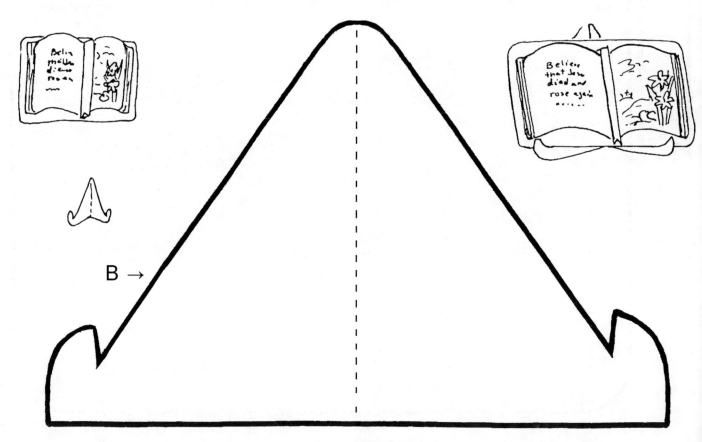

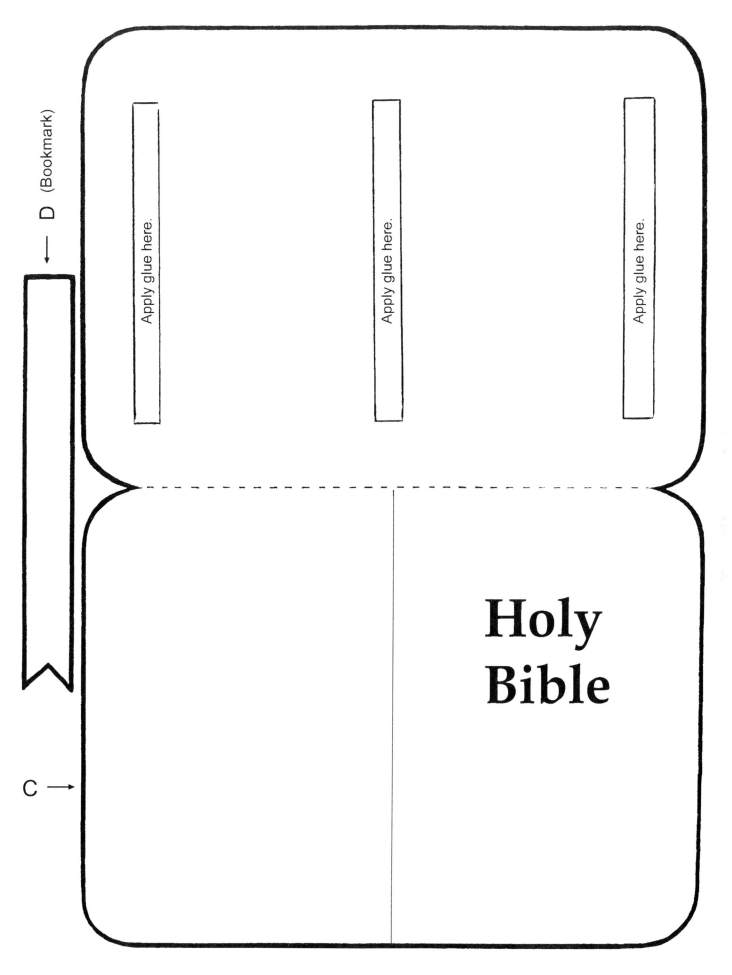

D (Bookmark)

Apply glue here.

Apply glue here.

Apply glue here.

C →

Holy Bible

49. Heart Poster

1. Color project.
2. Cut out on outside edge.
3. Punch out holes with a paper punch.
4. Glue to a 9″ x 12″ red construction paper.
5. Hang up.

50. Easter Banner

1. Color leaves green, banner blue, and lily centers white.
2. Make two copies of page 118 to use as top and bottom sections of the banner.
3. Cut out all project pieces.
4. Glue top banner section to bottom banner section (page 118).
5. Glue Bible verse on banner in area marked.
6. Fold leaves on dotted lines and glue back of folded areas on places marked on the banner.
7. Form the lily flowers by rolling flower in a cone shape and glue tab. Fold flower centers on dotted lines. Glue into middle of flowers. Fluff a little to look more realistic.
8. Glue flowers in the triangle shapes on the banner.
9. Fold back banner on double-dotted lines. Apply glue on the back area marked with ** and fasten. Insert two 8″ lengths of wooden dowels or 2 full-length, unsharpened pencils.
10. Tie a 15″ string or yarn to ends of top dowel.
11. Hang up.

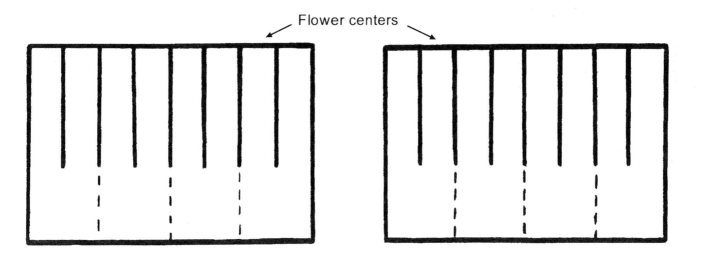

Flower centers

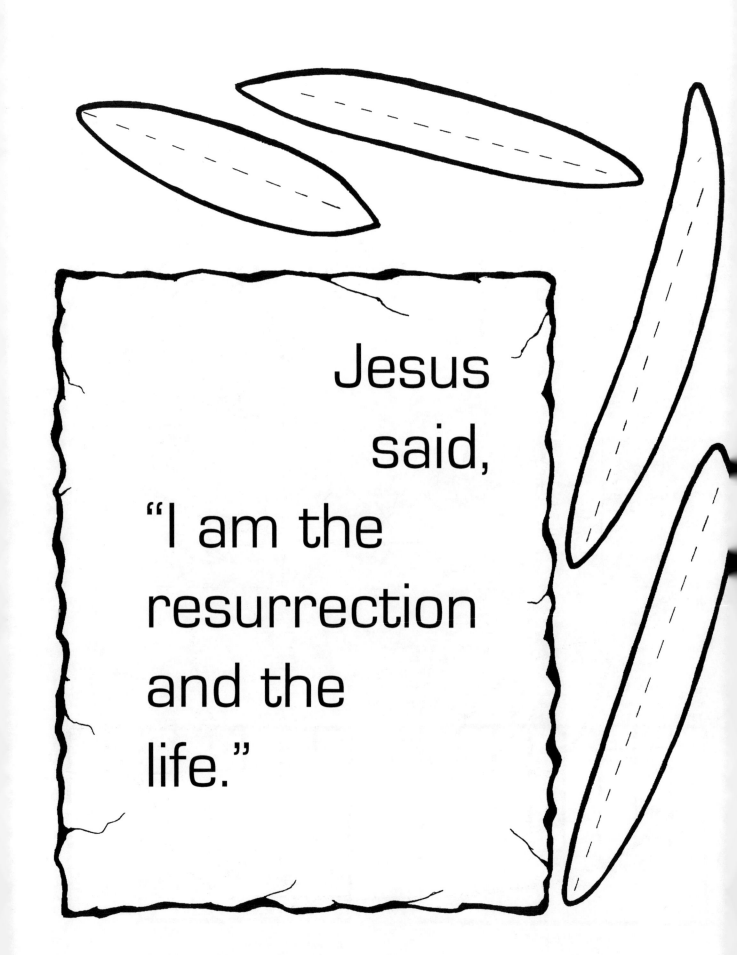

Jesus
said,

"I am the
resurrection
and the
life."

tab

tab

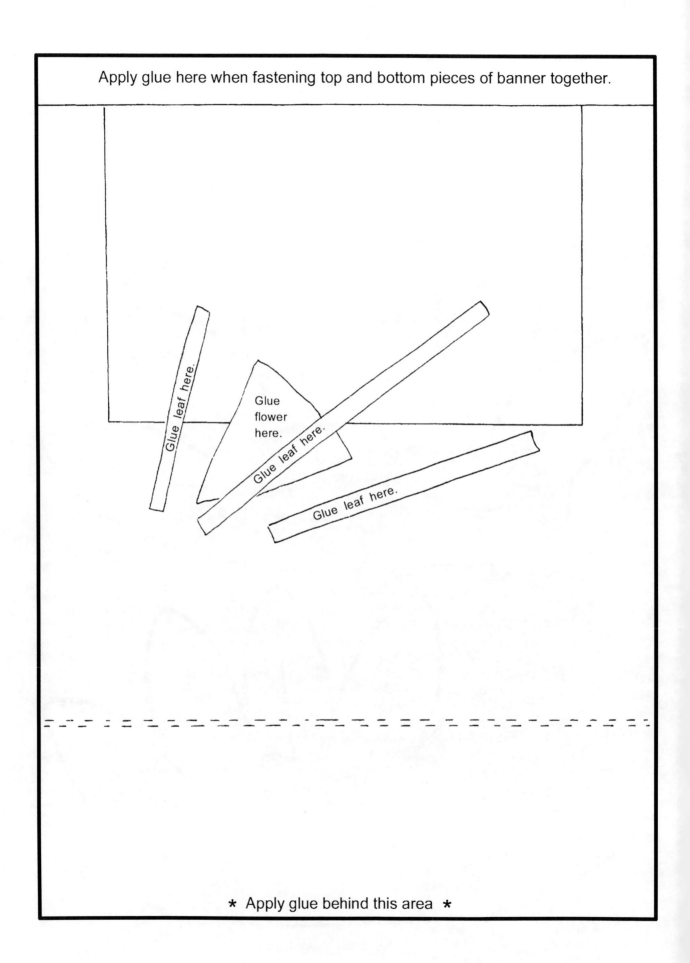

Apply glue here when fastening top and bottom pieces of banner together.

Glue leaf here.

Glue
flower
here.

Glue leaf here.

Glue leaf here.

* Apply glue behind this area *

Christian Light Publications, Inc., is a nonprofit conservative Mennonite publishing company providing Christ-centered, Biblical literature in a variety of forms including Gospel tracts, books, Sunday school materials, summer Bible school materials, and a full curriculum for Christian day schools and homeschools.

For more information at no obligation or for spiritual help, please write to us at:

Christian Light Publications, Inc.
P. O. Box 1212
Harrisonburg, VA 22801
Telephone: (540) 434-0768